LEARNING TO SEE
INTO THE
SPIRITUAL WORLD

D1545890

LEARNING TO SEE INTO THE SPIRITUAL WORLD

Lectures to the Workers at the Goetheanum

JUNE 28 – JULY 18, 1923

RUDOLF STEINER

Translated by
Walter Stuber and Mark Gardner

2009
ANTHROPOSOPHIC PRESS
STEINERBOOKS

Anthroposophic Press / SteinerBooks
610 Main Street, Great Barrington MA 01230
www.steinerbooks.org

The four lectures in this book constitute lectures eight to eleven
of *Rhythmen im Kosmos und im Menschenwesen; Wie Kommt
man zum Schauen der geistigen Welt?* (GA 350), published by
Rudolf Steiner Verlag, Dornach, Switzerland 1980.

Library of Congress Cataloging-in-Publication Data

Steiner, Rudolf, 1861-1925
[Wie kommt man zum Schauen der geistigen Welt? English]
Learning to see into the spiritual world : lectures to the workers
at the Goetheanum, June 28-July 18, 1923 / by Rudolf Steiner :
translated by Walter Stuber and Mark Gardner
    p. cm.
Translation of: Wie kommt man zum Schauen der geistigen Welt?
ISBN 0-88010-281-0
ISBN 978-0-88010-281-0
1. Anthroposophy. 2. Spirits. I. Title.
BP595.S894W54 1990
299'.935—dc20
                                                    89-49659
                                                         CIP

Printed in the United States of America

Contents

LEARNING TO SEE
INTO THE
SPIRITUAL WORLD

I

THE DEVELOPMENT OF INDEPENDENT THINKING AND OF THE ABILITY TO THINK BACKWARD

JUNE 28, 1923

A FEW QUESTIONS were put to me last time. I will now answer them, but in a somewhat different order than they were asked. The questions are:

What is the relationship between coming to see the secrets of the universe and one's conception of the world and of life?

How far must one go before one finds higher worlds on the path of natural science?

Do forces from the cosmos influence the whole of humanity?

What connection do plants have with the human being and the human body?

These are, of course, very complicated questions and so I would like to organize my remarks in such a way that the answers emerge gradually. One cannot do otherwise with such complicated questions because if you ask, How can I come to see the secrets of the universe?—this means, How can I arrive at a true spiritual science? Now, you must not imagine that this is something easy to do nowadays. Most people, when they hear that something like

Anthroposophy or spiritual science exists, think to themselves: Very well, if that is so, I too will acquire for myself the capacity to see the spirit. I will manage it within a week; then I will be able to know everything for myself. Needless to say, it is not as simple as that. One has to realize that a great deal is required to master even ordinary science. In order to undertake the simplest observations, one must first learn how to use the instruments. Of course it is comparatively easy to use a microscope, but if one wants to investigate something with the help of a microscope one cannot simply say: I will now put a piece of muscle or the like under the microscope and look into it; then I will know what goes on in the muscle. If you were to proceed like that, you would see nothing. To see something under a microscope, one must first prepare the slides. A piece of muscle is no use by itself: one must make very thin slices with a fine razor, and sometimes a little must be removed and another cut made so that finally one has a very thin film. And very often even then the microscope does not help. For if you have such a sliver of muscle or cell under the microscope, you will probably still see nothing. What one must do is ask oneself: How can I make visible what is under the microscope? Then, often, what one must next do is color what one wants to see with certain dyes to make it visible. But then one must realize one has changed something. One has to know how it would be if one had not changed it. But these things are still really quite simple.

If one wants to observe the stars with a telescope one must first learn how to handle a telescope, although this is much simpler than a microscope. You know there are people who set up telescopes in the streets for people to look through. By itself, this does not help much. For this again requires lenses and a clock, which in turn one must then also learn to handle, etc. These are only examples to show you how complicated it is to investigate the simplest things in the physical world.

Now, to investigate the spiritual world is really much more difficult, for more preparation is necessary. People imagine they can learn to do it in a week. But this is not so. Above all, one must realize that one has to activate something one has within oneself. What ordinarily is not active must be made active.

To make things clear for you I must explain that in all investigation of the spiritual world, as in normal science, one must frequently start with some knowledge of what is not normal. You can only learn how things really are if you know how they are when they are not normal. I once gave you a particular example of this. We have to consider this because people in the outside world call people mad who investigate the spiritual world, however normal they may be. We must therefore set about our investigations in such a way that in the end we arrive at the truth. Of course one must not think one can achieve anything by concerning oneself overmuch with what is diseased and abnormal, but one can learn much from it.

For instance, there are people who are not normal because they are, as is said, mentally deranged. What does this mean? There is no worse word in the world than "mentally deranged" (*geistesgestört*) for the spirit can never be deranged. Consider the following case for instance: If a man is deranged for twenty years—this happens—and afterward recovers, what has occurred? Perhaps for twenty years this person says that he is being persecuted by others—that he suffers, as one says, from paranoia—or he says that he sees all kinds of specters and apparitions which are not there, etc. This can continue for twenty years. Now this person who has been deranged for twenty years can become normal again. But in such cases you will always notice one thing. The man who was deranged for three, five or twenty years and recovers, will not be quite the same as before. Above all you will notice that he will tell you, after he has recovered, that throughout the time he was ill he was able to look into the spiritual world. He will tell you all sorts of things that he saw in the spiritual world. If one then pursues the matter with the knowledge one has gained of the spiritual world as a completely healthy person, one finds that some of what he says is rubbish but that also much of it is correct. This is what is so strange, someone can be deranged for twenty years, recover, and then tell you that he has been in the spiritual world and has experienced these things. And if one knows the spiritual world as a healthy, normal person, one must admit that he is right in many instances. If you speak to him during his mental illness, he will never be able to tell you anything sensible. He will tell you the nonsense he experiences. People who are mentally disturbed over a long period do not actually experience the spiritual world during their illness. They have not experienced anything of the spiritual world. But after they have recovered they can, in a certain way, look back to the time they were ill, and what they have not experienced appears to them like glimpses into the spiritual world. This conviction that they have seen much of the spiritual world only appears when they have recovered.

One can learn much from this. One can learn that the human being contains something that is not used at all during the time he or she is insane. But it was there, it was alive. And where was it? It was not in the outer world, for the person told you that the sky was red and the clouds green—all kinds of things. The sick person saw nothing properly in the outer world. But the inner being, which the person cannot use in the deranged state, is in the spiritual world. When the person can use the brain again and can look back on what the spiritual being lived through, then spiritual experiences come.

From this we see that a human being who is mentally ill lives spiritually in the spiritual world. The spirit in the person is perfectly healthy. What, then, is ill in a mentally ill patient? It is, in fact, the body: the body cannot use the soul and spirit. When a person is called mentally ill, there is always something ill in the body, and obviously when the brain is ill one cannot think properly. In the same way, when the liver is ill, one cannot feel properly.

This is why "mentally ill" (*geisteskrank*) is the most incorrect expression that one can use, for "mentally ill" does not mean that the spirit (*geist*) is ill. It means the body is so ill that it cannot use the spirit which is always healthy. Above all you must be quite clear that the spirit is always healthy. Only the body can become ill, with the result that it cannot use the spirit in the right way. When someone has a diseased brain it is like having a hammer that breaks with every blow. If I say to someone who does not have a hammer, You are a lazy fellow, you are not even able to strike a blow—then this is, of course, nonsense. He could well strike a blow, but he does not have a hammer. It is therefore nonsense to say someone is mentally ill. The spirit is perfectly healthy, only it lacks the body through which to act.

A good example of what one can learn in this way comes from considering how our thinking works. From what I have told you, you will see that, though one has the spirit, one needs a tool for thinking, and this is the brain. In the physical world one needs the brain. It is not particularly clever of materialism to propose that one needs a brain. Obviously one needs a brain. But this postulate explains nothing about the spirit. We can also learn that the spirit can completely withdraw itself. In the case of mental illness the spirit does withdraw completely. And it is important to know this, because this shows that people today—and now I am going to tell you something that will really surprise you—cannot think at all. They delude themselves that they can think, but they cannot. I will show you why people cannot think.

You will object: But people go to school; nowadays one already learns to think quite well even in grade school. So it seems, at least. Nevertheless, people today cannot think at all. It only appears as if they could. In grade school we have grade school teachers. They have also learned something; ostensibly they have also learned to think. Those from whom they have learned have, as one says in Stuttgart, "swollen heads." These are very clever people according to present ideas. They have been to a university. Before they went to university they went to high school. There they learned Latin. If you think back a bit you might say: But my teacher did not know Latin. Perhaps not, but your teacher learned from teachers who did. And what they learned was entirely under the influence of the Latin language. Everything one learns today is under the influence of the Latin language. You can see this from the fact that when you are given a prescription, it is written in Latin. It stems from the time when everything was written in Latin. It is not so long ago, only thirty to forty years, that if one went to university one was obliged to write one's thesis in Latin. Everything one learns today in schools is under the influence of Latin. This is because in the Middle Ages, up to the fourteenth and fifteenth centuries—this is not so long ago—all teaching was in Latin. For instance the first person to lecture in German was a certain Thomasius[1] in Leipzig. This was not long ago, it was in the seventeenth century. Before that lectures were given in Latin. In the Middle Ages everything was in Latin and everybody who wanted to learn anything in school had to go through the Latin language; if one wanted to learn anything new one had to learn Latin first. You may protest: But surely not in the grade schools. But there were no grade schools before the sixteenth century. Only gradually, as the vernacular was adopted by science, did grade schools come into existence. So, you see, Latin influences our whole thinking. All of you think like people who have learned to think under the influence of Latin. And if you were to say that the Americans, for instance, could not have learned Latin so long ago—well, today's Americans emigrated from Europe! They too depended on the Latin language.

Latin has a certain peculiarity. It was developed in ancient Rome in such a way that it thinks by itself. It is interesting how Latin is taught in high schools. One learns Latin; and then one learns thinking, correct thinking according to Latin syntax. So one's whole way of thinking does not depend on anything one does, but on what the Latin language does. You understand, don't you, that this is something quite significant. People today who have learned in schools do not think for themselves: the Latin language thinks in them, even if they have not learned Latin. Strange as it is, one meets independent thinking today only in the few people who have not been to school very much.

I am not suggesting that we return to illiteracy. We cannot do this. In no area do I advocate going backward, but one must understand how things have become as they are. Therefore it is important to be able to go back to what simple people know, though they have not had much schooling. They are not very forthcoming because they are used to being laughed at. In spite of everything, it is important to know that contemporary human beings do not think for themselves, but that the Latin language thinks in them.

You see, as long as one cannot think for oneself, one can in no way enter the spiritual world. This is the reason why modern science is opposed to all spiritual knowledge; because through Latin education people can no longer think for themselves. This is the first thing to learn—independent thinking. People are quite right when they say: the brain thinks. Why does the brain think? Because Latin syntax goes into the brain, and the brain thinks quite automatically in modern humanity. What we see are automatons of the Latin language who do not think for themselves.

In recent years something remarkable has happened. I hinted at it last time, but you may not have noticed it, because it is not easy to see. Something remarkable has happened in recent years. Now, as you know, besides the physical body, we have the etheric body. (I will not speak for the moment of the rest.) The brain belongs to the physical body. The etheric body is also in the brain, and one can think independently only with the etheric body. One cannot think independently with the physical body. One can think with the physical body only when—as under the influence of Latin—the brain is used like an automaton. But as long as one thinks only with the brain, one cannot think anything spiritual. To think something spiritual one must start to think with the etheric body— with the etheric body which, as in the case of the mentally ill, is often not used for years. It has to be awakened to an inner activity.

This is the first thing one has to learn: to think independently. Without independent thinking, one cannot enter the spiritual world. But it is, of course, necessary first of all to find out that one has not learned to think for oneself in one's youth! One has learned to think only what has been thought for centuries through the use of the Latin language. And if one really grasps this then one knows that the first condition for entry into the spiritual world is this: Learn to think independently!

Now we come to what I wanted to point out when I said that in recent times something remarkable has happened. The people who, more than anyone else, thought along Latin lines were the people of learning—those who, for instance, created physics. They worked it out with thoughts derived from Latin and with the physical brain.

When we were young—when I was about the same age as young E. here—we learned physics, which was worked out with a Latin brain. We learned only what was thought out with a Latin brain. Since then a lot has happened. When I was young the telephone was just being invented. Until then it did not exist. After this followed all the other great inventions that everyone now takes for granted as if they had always been there. But these inventions appeared only in the last decades. This caused more and more people to become involved in science who were not Latin trained. This is rather a strange thing. When one looks into the scientific life of the last decades one finds more and more technicians of this kind involved in science. These people did not have much to do with Latin and so their thinking did not become so automatic. And this non-automatic thinking was then picked up by others. This is why today physics is full of concepts and ideas that fall apart. This is most interesting. There is, for instance, Professor Gruner[2] in Bern, who two years ago spoke about the new direction in physics. He said that all the concepts have changed in the last years.

The reason that one does not notice this is because if you listen to lectures on popular science, people tell you what was thought thirty years ago. They cannot tell you what is thought today because they themselves cannot think that way yet. If you take the thoughts of thirty years ago as valid, it is just like taking a piece of ice and melting it; the ideas melt away. They are no longer there if one wants to follow them exactly. We must see this. If you had learned physics thirty years ago and now see what has become of it today, you would want to tear your hair out because you would have to admit: I cannot handle all this with the concepts I have learned. This is how it is. And why? Because in recent years, through the development of humanity, the human being has reached the point when the etheric body is supposed to begin to think, and human beings do not want this to happen. They want to go on thinking with the physical body. Concepts fall apart in the physical body, and yet human beings do not want to learn to think with the etheric body. They do not want to think independently.

Now you see why, in the year 1893, it became necessary for me to write the book *The Philosophy of Spiritual Activity*.[3] It is not the contents of this book that are so important, though obviously at that time I wished to tell the world what is said in it, but the most important thing is that independent thinking appeared in this book for the first time. No one can possibly understand this book who does not think independently. From the beginning, page by page, readers must become accustomed to using their etheric body if they would think the thoughts in this book at all. Hence this book is a means of education—a very important means—and must be taken up as such.

When this book appeared in the nineties people did not know at all what to make of it. It was as if someone in Europe wrote Chinese and no one could understand it. It was of course written in German, but people were completely unaccustomed to the thoughts expressed in it because all connection with Latin was purposely cast off. For the very first time, quite consciously, it was intended that there should be no thoughts in it that are influenced by Latin, but only independent thoughts. Only the physical brain is a Latin scholar. The etheric body is no Latin scholar. And therefore one has to try to express such thoughts in a language one can have only in the etheric body.

I will tell you something else. People have noticed, of course, that concepts have changed in the last decades. When I was young the professor filled the whole blackboard with writing. You had to learn it all and then you did well in your exams. But recently, people have begun to notice what Gruner said in his inaugural lecture: none of our concepts would remain valid if there were no solid bodies, only fluids. If the whole world were liquid, as Gruner imagined in his lecture, then our concepts would be invalid and we would have to think quite differently.

Yes, of course one would have to think differently if there were no solid bodies. In that case you, as you sit here, could do nothing with the concepts you learned in school. If you—say, as a fish—suddenly became clever and had the idea that, as a fish, you wanted to attend a human university, then you would learn something that does not exist for a fish, because it lives in water. A fish only has a boundary sensation of a solid body; the moment it touches the body, it is immediately repulsed. So, if a fish began to think, it would have to have thoughts quite different from those a human being has. But human beings likewise need such different thoughts, because other thoughts escape them, so that they have to say to themselves: If everything were liquid I would have to have quite different thoughts. And, well, have I not told you about the condition of the Earth when there were no solid bodies and when everything was fluid, even the animals? I have told you of this condition before. Can you not then understand that present-day thinking cannot reach back to these conditions? It cannot think them. So present-day thinking cannot make anything of the beginning of the world. Naturally, then, people today begin to say to themselves: Good heavens! If the world were fluid we would have to have quite different concepts. But in the spiritual world there are no solid bodies. So, with all the concepts with which Latin has gradually schooled us, we are unable to enter the spiritual world. We must wean ourselves of these concepts.

Here is another hidden truth. In Greek times, which preceded the Latin era (the Latin era began only in the fifth or sixth century b.c., but the Greek period is much older), there still was knowledge of the spirit. One could still see into the spiritual world. This was gradually extinguished when Rome emerged with the Latin language. Now I must again say something you will find curious, but you will understand it. Who has used Latin, only Latin, throughout the centuries? More than anyone, the Church. It is precisely the Church, which claims to teach humanity about the spirit, that has contributed the most to drive out the spirit. In the Middle Ages all universities were ecclesiastical. Of course, one must be grateful to the Church for founding the universities in the thirteenth and fourteenth centuries; but it founded them in Latin, and Latin thought has no possibility of attaining the spirit. And so it gradually came about that we have concepts relating only to solid bodies. Just look at the Romans, they introduced only dry, prosaic and unspiritual concepts into the world. And this is the reason that all ideas became so material. How would the Greeks have described the sacrament of the Eucharist? They would certainly not have described it as if the elements were actually blood and flesh. This stems from materialism. So even the concept of the Eucharist has become materialistic, and this is connected with the Latin language.

Latin is entirely logical. I have worked with many people who, although they were German, were Latin in their whole attitude to life. If one wanted to make something clear to them, one quickly translated it into Latin, because since the time of Christ only in Latin does one think logically. But this logical thinking applies only to solid bodies. If one wants to enter the spiritual world one needs fluid concepts.

There is, for instance, the Theosophical Society, which also wanted to reach into the spiritual world. The Theosophical Society says that the human being has a physical body, an etheric body, etc. But these thoughts are materialistic because they describe the physical body as dense, the etheric body as a little thinner, and the astral body thinner still. But all these are still bodies, they never become spirit. If one wants to reach the spirit one has to find concepts that are constantly changing. Even when I draw something on the blackboard you will notice that I take this into consideration. When I draw the physical body I try to portray human physical body as it is. But if I try to draw the etheric body, I would never dream of representing it in the same way. I would do it like this. (See the following page.) The human being has an etheric body that expands.

But you must know that this is not so much the etheric body, but the picture of one instant. In the next moment it is different. So if I wish to draw the etheric body, I would have to draw, quickly wipe it off, draw differently, again wipe it off, draw again and wipe it off. It is in constant movement. With the concepts we have today, we cannot catch up with these movements. This is what you have to

keep in mind, concepts must become mobile. People must get into the habit of it. This is why it is necessary that thinking become completely independent.

But this is not enough. I will tell you something more. As you know, human beings develop, but one does not usually notice it. However, when a person is quite young, one does notice it. One knows that a child who is only four years old can neither write nor read nor do addition. An eight-year-old child can perhaps do these things. Here one can see development. But in later life, when we have made our way, we might wish to appear as if we are so very superior that we don't admit that we can still develop. But we do develop, throughout our lives, and it is remarkable how we do so. Our development goes like this: Imagine this is the human being—I will draw this diagrammatically:

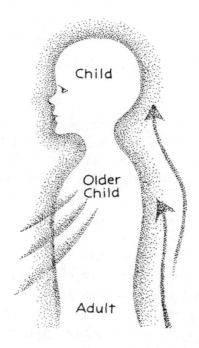

When a child is quite young the development proceeds from the head. After the change of teeth, the development proceeds from the chest. Therefore, one must watch how a child between seven and fourteen is breathing—that the child breathes adequately, etc. So this is a picture of the older child. (Nowadays one would have to say it differently. Children do not like to be called children any more. From fourteen onward one must call them "young ladies" and "young gentlemen.") Only at puberty does the development proceed from the limbs and from the whole human being. So one can say that only when one has reached puberty is one developing from the whole being. And this goes on throughout our twenties and thirties. But when one becomes older—some of you can already see it in yourselves—there is a certain retrogression. This need not be the case if one has adopted a spiritual mode of life, but in normal life there is a certain retrogression as one gets older. It is just the task of Anthroposophy to see to it that in the future one does not regress as one gets older. Slowly and gradually this must happen.

Now there are people whose mental capacities diminish alarmingly. But the mind, the spirit, cannot diminish. It is again only the body. It is interesting that often it is the most brilliant people who regress very much in old age. You may have heard that Kant was reckoned to be one of the wisest men, but in old age he became feeble-minded. His body regressed so much that he could not express his wise mind any more. And so it often is. Especially the very intelligent become feeble-minded in old age. It is an exaggerated form of what happens to everybody. Eventually in old age there comes a point when one can no longer use the physical body. The reason for this is mainly that the arteries harden with excessive deposits of calcium. And the more this happens, the less one can make use of the physical body. As, up to the fortieth year, development proceeds from the head into the whole body, so, in the same degree, the process reverses. As one proceeds from the forties to the fifties one comes back to using the chest more, and in old age one goes back to using the head. So if one becomes really old, one again has to use one's head much more. But then one would have to use the finer head—the etheric head. But this is not learned in Latin education. And it is just those who, in the last decades, had a materialistic Latin education who are most strongly affected by senility.

In old age one must go back to childhood. There are people in whom this is very noticeable. They become mentally weaker and weaker. However, the mind itself, the spirit, remains completely intact; it is only the physical body that becomes weaker and weaker. In the end, such people can no longer do the things they first learned to do in life. Such things happen. Let us say a man gets old. Then he can no longer do the work he used to do. He can do only what he did as an older child. Finally he cannot even do this. He can only play, and he understands only ideas he learned when playing as a young child. There are even very old people who can understand only what their parents or their nurse told them in the very first years of their life. The saying about returning to second childhood is well founded. One really does return to childhood.

Actually it is not a misfortune, that is, if one has developed a spiritual life. In fact it is rather fortunate, for as long as one is a child, one can use one's etheric body. If a child runs about and shouts and does all kinds of things, this is not done by the physical body—except if the child has a stomachache, but even then the stomachache has to be transferred to the etheric and astral bodies, so that the child thrashes around as a result. What tears around is not the physical body. Then, one grows old and returns to childhood. Gradually one has learned to not tear around any more. One no longer uses the etheric body as a child does, but for something more sensible. So it can be fortunate that one returns to childhood.

This is the second point. The first was that in order to enter the spiritual world one has to learn to think in the right way. We shall have to speak further about how one achieves this. The matter is very complicated. Today we will concentrate on the question of why there has to be independent thinking. One must break away from much in our modern education, for what one learns in modern education is not independent thinking, it is Latin thinking. Do not imagine that the thinking emerging from socialist theories being developed today is free thinking! It has all been learned from what originally came from Latin, but people do not know it. Workers may have this or that intention in their will, but when they think, they think in bourgeois concepts, which originate in Latin thinking. So the first thing one has to learn is independent thinking. The second thing is that one must learn to live not only in the present moment, but to be able to turn back to the life one led in childhood. If you want to penetrate into the spiritual world you must be able to remember how it was when you were twelve years old. What did you do? One must not do this superficially, but imagine it in great detail. Nothing is better than to begin to try to picture: Oh yes, there I was twelve years old—I can see it quite clearly—there was a pile of stones by the roadside and I climbed up on it. Once I fell off. There was a hazel bush and I took out my pocket knife and cut off some branches and cut my finger. It is important to really visualize what one did so many years ago; in this way one gets away from living just in the present. If you think the way one learns to think today, you think with your present physical body. But if you turn back to when you were twelve, you cannot think with your physical body as it then was, for it is no longer there, and so you must think with your etheric body. (I have told you before that the physical body is renewed every seven years.) If you think back to something that happened at twelve or fourteen, you call on your etheric body. This is the way to call up inner activity.

Above all, one should get accustomed to thinking in a new way, different from one's usual thinking. How do you think? You know we met here at nine o'clock. I began by reading to you the questions on the slips of paper. Then I proceeded with various observations, and we have now arrived at saying that we must think back into the life we lived when we were twelve or fourteen years old. When you get home, you can, if you find it interesting, think through these thoughts again. One can do this. Many people do it. They will go through the thoughts once again. But you can do something different. You can ask yourself: What did he say last? The last thing he said was that one should think back to one's early life, to the age of twelve or fourteen years. Before that he said one must have independent thinking. Earlier still he described how Latin gradually took over. And before that, how a person who has been mentally ill for a time and then recovers and looks back on it, says he has experienced extraordinary things. It was further explained to us how the inner being cannot be mentally ill, only the body can be ill. —Thus, you have run backward through the whole lecture.

But in the world things do not run backward. I could possibly have given you the lecture backward in the first place, but then you would not have understood it. One has to begin at the beginning and then look at the whole as it gradually unfolds, but once one has understood it, one can think it backward. But things do not run backward. So you tear yourself free from things and say: Just to be contrary, I will think things exactly not the way they go in the outer world, but I will think them backward. This requires a certain strength. When one thinks backward one makes the self inwardly active. A person who wants to see through a telescope has to learn how to handle it. In the same way, one who wants to see into the spiritual world must learn how to handle it. One must think backward many times and then the moment will come when one knows: Ah, now I am entering the spiritual world.

You see, throughout your whole life you have accustomed your physical body to thinking forward, not backward. When you begin to think backward your physical body does not take part in it. Something strange happens. This is the first advice to those who ask: How can I reach the spiritual world? You can also read this in *Knowledge of the Higher Worlds and its Attainment.*[4] What is said there repeatedly is: At least learn to go backward through the course of the day; then other things. People have, of course, learned to think only with their physical body. They notice this and have to make a great effort to think backward, but they have learned to think only with the physical body, not with the etheric body. Now there is an all-out strike by the etheric body; yes, a real "general strike." And if people would not fall asleep so easily, they would know that if they began to think backward, they would arrive at the spiritual world. But the moment the vision begins, they fall asleep. People fall asleep, because the effort is too great. So one must exert one's entire will and all one's strength not to fall asleep. In addition, one must have patience. Sometimes it takes years, but one must have patience. If somebody could tell you what you experienced unconsciously when you went to sleep after thinking backward, you would see that it was something very wise. The most simple-minded people have extraordinarily wise thoughts in their sleep, but they do not know anything about it.

So today I have drawn your attention to the fact that one must first learn to think independently. Well, one can do this. I will not say that only my *Philosophy of Spiritual Activity* serves this purpose, but it was quite consciously written in a way that would lead to independent thinking. Independent thinking; thinking backward accurately over things that happened when you were ten or twelve years old, or over other things you have experienced—with these we have at least begun to describe how one tears oneself free from the physical body and how one finds one's way into the spiritual world.

I will pursue this further and eventually deal with all four questions.

2

The Uses of What Seems Boring:
The Spiritual World as the
Inverse of the Physical

June 30, 1923

I will now continue to answer the questions I took up last time. You must be quite clear that the answers to these questions are among the most difficult. I will try to make them as easy as possible. I have already mentioned that, to find a way to spiritual vision, first one must become accustomed to completely independent thinking. Second, one must have the ability to think backward. You must therefore attempt to think backward the things that normally occur in daily life in a 1, 2, 3, sequence. For instance, as I told you last time I give a lecture, you should try to think it through backward, from the end to the beginning. These two aspects constitute the absolute first steps.

In connection with the second question I want to explain something else. As you know, a human being can live only within a specific temperature range. When it becomes very hot in the summer, one sweats but can still tolerate it. However, were it to become progressively hotter, a point would be reached when one would no longer be able to live. Similarly, a human being can tolerate a given degree of cold, and if it gets colder than that, one freezes.

The fact is that one cannot see spiritual beings between the two extremes within which the human body lives: i.e., between the cold at which one freezes and the heat that is still barely tolerable. Within these extremes, where human life is possible, we cannot see spiritual beings. It is not surprising therefore that one cannot perceive spiritual beings when one is in the body.

As I told you last time, when we begin to think backward and approach the point of consciously seeing spiritual beings, we often fall asleep. Most people go to sleep, unless they have trained themselves to stay awake.

Also, spiritual beings are perceived at higher temperatures than are normally tolerable to us. One could see spiritual beings at high temperatures, but of course one cannot tolerate those temperatures. At low temperatures, likewise, one could perceive spiritual beings, if one could transform oneself into a snow-being, but then one would freeze in the process. Thus, what seems unlikely to people is actually a fact: spiritual beings withdraw themselves from the temperatures that are tolerable to us in our physical body.

While human beings cannot tolerate those temperatures in the body, they can tolerate them in the soul; but, of course, the soul goes to sleep. The soul does not freeze, the soul does not burn, the soul goes to sleep.

There are, however, circumstances whereby one can have an inkling as to what goes on in the extreme temperatures outside those one ordinarily lives in. I will give you an example. When one has a fever, one reaches inwardly a temperature that one cannot bear. One does not immediately reach so high a temperature that one dies—because the warmth is created from within, one is able to bear it. However, when the fever enters these higher temperatures one may speak in a way that is not normal on the earth.

What people babble in their fever has no relation to what we are used to on earth. Now, the materialist may say: Yes, but there are nevertheless untrue thoughts produced that are cooked up in the heat of fever.

A person entering into a state of high temperature, first of all feels feverish, then speaks nonsense. The soul cannot speak nonsense. Even when the soul is living in a high fever, it cannot speak nonsense. It seems or appears to speak nonsense at higher bodily temperatures because the body is not in order.

You can verify the truth of this by the following example. Let us think about our experience with those glass spheres one sometimes finds in flower gardens—a sphere that is actually a kind of mirror in which the environment is reflected. If you look at yourself in one of these, you will find yourself with a face that you would rather not have in reality. [He sketched this.] You would hate to have that kind of face. However, you will not say: Oh no! What kind of a thing did I turn into? You would not believe that this is really your own face, just because it looks changed in the sphere. Similarly, if your soul talks nonsense when you have a fever, you will not say that your soul is talking nonsense; but rather you will assume that whatever is said by your soul seems nonsensical because it is spoken out of a brain that is sick—just as your face looks distorted and flattened out because it is reflected by a false mirror. So you must say to yourself: When I have a fever and speak nonsense, it is my soul that is speaking through a sick brain. When I see myself reflected in a glass sphere, it is not that I have another face, but that my face appears distorted. In the same way, the speech of someone who is sick with a fever appears distorted because it is spoken out of a sick body and a brain that is not working properly.

Now, we might ask why the brain does not work properly? It is because the whole blood circulation is too fast. You can verify this by feeling your pulse when you have a fever. The blood circulation produces warmth which rises to the head—you feel a fever—and your soul now appears reflected as by a distorted mirror.

The opposite can also happen, but this will not happen as a result of lying in the snow and letting oneself freeze, because then one would actually die of freezing. This opposite experience can happen, but only as the result of something spiritual.

We come now to a strange subject. Carefully consider the following: Let's assume one begins to concentrate, to think powerfully about the smallest things (it is better to think about the small things that most people wouldn't even want to give time to)—for example, a triangle. Let us say we have a triangle, and we divide it into four equal parts so that we have four equal triangles. [He draws on the blackboard.]

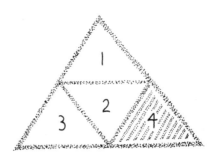

You can see that the whole triangle is greater than the four smaller triangles. From this I can make a general statement: The whole is greater than the parts. [He writes the sentence on the blackboard.] But now let's assume that a well-fed stockbroker comes by and I tell him, Hey, just think, the whole is greater than its parts. He will say, No, that is too boring for me. He would say it again if I continued to speak to him and said that the blackboard is a physical body with a given size and extension, the table is also a body with a given size and extension, and I then constructed the general statement: All bodies have extension—are extended in space. [He writes the sentence on the blackboard.]

If a whole conference was given to you, or if a lecture was given, consisting in the single statement: All bodies have extension, you would walk away, saying, Gosh, that was boring!

Let's say I made other obvious remarks to you, for instance: the meadow is green, the rose is red, these things have colors; and yesterday there was a trial in court where the judge passed judgment, but the judgment had no color, and then I went to another place where there also was a trial and a judgment, and it had no color either. And therefore I said: Judgments have no color. [He writes the sentence on the blackboard.]

Let's assume someone stood in front of you for an hour and told you: Judgments have no color. You would think to yourself, I have spent a whole hour listening to someone bore me. This is the ultimate boredom. But why are these statements so boring? I should not be telling them to you humorously; I should be standing before you stiff and severe like a professor, announcing: Today we will consider the statement: Judgments have no color. And then, of course, I would have to lecture to you for a whole hour to prove that judgments have no color; all bodies have extension; etc.

I could also give you another instance: draw a line from one point to another; this is a straight line. All others are curved, and when you look at it you would immediately say the straight line is the shortest way; all others are longer. Here again I could write down a general statement: A straight line is the shortest distance between two points. Again, if I were to speak for a whole hour on the subject, you would find it exceedingly boring.

The whole is greater than its parts.

All bodies have extension.

Judgments have no color.

A straight line is the shortest distance between two points.

There is a German professor who said that it is quite possible to perceive things of the spiritual world, but that the only things that we can perceive of the spiritual world are what reside in such statements as: the whole is greater than its parts; judgments have no color; bodies are extended; a straight line is the shortest distance between two points. This, he says, is all one can know of the spiritual world. Of course, most students are extremely bored by his lectures. It is also the case that people today have come to believe that science has to be boring, and therefore many of the students are actually excited by this professor! —This, of course, is just an aside.

The real story is the following. Taken by themselves, statements such as "the whole is greater than its parts" and "a straight line is the shortest distance between two points" cause the back of our head to become cold. This is what usually happens: the temperature drops and the area at the back of one's head becomes cold. When the temperature drops you begin to feel cold and you want to get away from such statements—they are so boring. This is a fact—boredom causes a drop in temperature at the back of the head—not in the whole body, but just at the back of the head. What cools the head down is not snow or ice but something of a spiritual nature, insofar as there are subjects that hold no interest for the human being.

It is of course possible to make fun of these statements, but the fact remains, that patiently to think such thoughts over and over again means to put oneself, again and again, deliberately into a state of dreadful boredom, and this is a good way to reach in the direction of a true spiritual perception. It is remarkable that the very things people do not want to do in general are the things they must practice if they wish to have a real look into the spiritual world. Mathematics for many is boring; it causes a drop in temperature at the back of the head; and precisely because it is a cold subject for most, and precisely because they have to work at it, those people who do, have the least trouble reaching into the spiritual world.

Those who overcome this resistance and experience again and again the truth of these statements are those who can create artificially a state of boredom in themselves. They will have the easiest way into the spiritual world.

I have told you already, when one has a fever one's pulse speeds up. One warms up, and this warmth reaches into the head and into the brain, and in this way the warmth causes one to talk nonsense. If, on the other hand, one struggles with such statements as we have mentioned, this causes one's blood to slow down, and there is an accumulation of salts deposited in the back of the brain. Most people react in one of two ways to this. Some get a stomachache and they notice this right away, as soon as they start to think of these statements, and so they stop. One can go on thinking, as, for example, Nietzsche did. He always tortured himself with such statements when he was a young man, and the salts accumulated in his head, and in his case he suffered dreadful migraines. The objective is to be able to think such thoughts without causing a migraine or a stomachache.

One must find a way to be completely healthy while at the same time artificially producing in oneself a state of boredom. Thus, someone who wanted to tell you quite honestly how to reach into the spiritual world would tell you first of all to learn how to create boredom artificially in yourself. Short of this you have no hope of reaching the spiritual world.

But look now at our contemporary world. What is it that people want at this time? People today are constantly trying to drive away boredom. Just look at all the things and all the places people run to in order not to be bored. They always want to be amused; but what does that mean, to want to be amused all the time? It means that they really want to run away from the spirit! It has no other meaning; and people today always want to be amused, which makes it clear that wherever anything spiritual might be present people of our time always run away from it immediately. People are not conscious of this, they do it unconsciously, but the fact remains that they want amusement and to run away from the spirit.

Well, only those can reach into the spirit who are not afraid of renouncing amusements and of living in such boring statements. When one can manage to live artificially in boring statements without getting a stomachache or a migraine, but can actually tolerate living in such statements for many hours at a time, then it becomes possible to contemplate the spiritual world.

Then, an additional change must take place in this act of holding oneself consciously in these statements. One notices, if one has been living with these statements for a while, that they start to turn around. If I think about the statement "the large triangle is greater than its parts" for a long time—if I think about it for a very long time—there comes a point when the statement somehow turns around. It even starts to become interesting, for I start to have the following perception: If I have a triangle here, and I consider one quarter of that triangle and take it out, it somehow begins to grow with me and it no longer remains true that the whole is greater than the parts. Suddenly that quarter part is larger for me, I see that it has grown, so that I now must say: The whole is smaller than the parts! [He writes this on the blackboard.] By doing this, I have worked myself into a position where I can see how things work in the spiritual world. Things there are the opposite of the way they are in the physical world.

In the physical world, the whole is always greater than its parts. In the spiritual world, the part is greater than the whole. It is impossible to understand a human being without knowing that the part is greater than the whole.

Contemporary science always wants to look at the smallest parts, the components of things. If, for example, we study the liver of a person, we find that it is smaller than the person in the physical realm. But if we start looking at it from a spiritual point of view, we find that it grows and grows to gigantic proportions; it actually becomes a whole world in itself. If one cannot see this, then it is impossible to perceive the liver at all in a spiritual way. Therefore you must first honestly arrive at the statement: The whole is smaller than the part, or the part is greater than the whole.

In the same way, if you think for a long time—if you think long enough—about the statement "all bodies have surfaces, or are extended," then there is a danger that the back of your brain will freeze. If you think upon this statement in this way, all the bodies shrivel into one; they stop having surfaces—external surfaces—and in the end you arrive at the statement "bodies do not have surfaces, they are not extended." [He writes the sentence on the blackboard.]

Now I will take an amusing example, amusing in the physical world, but of the highest seriousness in the spiritual world, where it could seem that there is nothing more foolish than to say: There was a trial in Buxtehude in which judgment was passed and it had no color; and in Trippstrill a judgment was passed in the course of a trial, and this also had no color. If you think about judgments for a long time, they in fact acquire color. Just as you can say the rose is red, so you can say the judgment in Buxtehude was a kind of dirty yellow, and the judgment in Trippstrill was red. There can even be some judgments that are a beautiful red, although this is rarely the case.

As you begin to understand this, you begin to grow into the statement: All judgments made by human beings have color. [He writes the sentence on the blackboard] Only now does one reach the point of being at all capable of thinking about the spiritual world, because it has the opposite characteristics of the physical world.

A straight line is the shortest path between two points. This is true to such an extent that all geometry is built upon it. It is one of the first statements in geometry. It is as true in the physical world as anything ever can be true in the physical world. But if one thinks about it differently— if some being goes from village A to village B, and that being is not a physical but a spiritual being, the way will seem very short if the being walks in a half circle. The statement then changes to: A straight line is the longest way between two points. [He writes this sentence on the blackboard.]

The whole is smaller than its parts.
No body has extension.
Judgments have color.
A straight line is the longest distance between two points.

You must admit there is something here that astonishes you, but the world as a whole does not like these kinds of things, and people will say: Someone who says that judgments have color must have a fever or he is mad! Of course, the whole point is that one reaches these things in full consciousness without the use of one's body. The spiritual world has characteristics that are the opposite of the physical world and one may come to this realization through the simplest statements, for the simplest statements are the hardest to believe.

As you know, if someone starts announcing interesting things about the spiritual world, everybody starts listening; for instance, if someone starts talking about ghosts. But if someone tells you first that you must get used to creating boredom in yourself artificially—it has to be artificially—this doesn't seem so interesting. If you are just naturally bored by external science, nothing comes of it; it has to be done artificially, through an inner effort that enables you to reach the state of boredom without getting a migraine or a stomachache. The body must not participate in that state of boredom. The moment your body is involved, it is clear that you will get a migraine or a stomachache. Don't listen when people tell you, Do not let professor so and so bore you. Such advice will be of no help, it will not make you see into the spiritual world. What you must do is gradually overcome both migraines and stomachaches.

You see, the student is sitting there—the professor bores him to death — he should be getting a stomachache or a migraine, but he doesn't. What happens in this case is that other organs come into play that do not hurt. People, in fact, do get sick when the physical body is involved in boredom. If you induce boredom in the way contemporary science does, it only makes people sick.

If one teaches people in the right way, one gives them the ability to produce, through their own powers, in total freedom, the boredom that, when penetrated, will gradually allow entrance to the spiritual world. One must take hold of absolutely basic judgments in the physical world and see how they are turned upside-down in the spiritual world.

There is one extremely good way in which it is possible to work on oneself. For example: let us say you have experienced something very boring, so boring that you walked away from it because it was so boring, so boring that you could not stand it anymore. (You were so happy when it was over!) In such a case it is important that you start very, very slowly thinking it through again. Let me tell you that I have learned a great deal from this kind of exercise in my life. When I was young, I listened to many dreadfully boring lectures; but before a boring lecture even started, I would look forward to it, because it brought about the kind of result sleep normally does in life. I was very happy. I would tell myself: You are going to listen to an hour of boring lecturing. When the lecture started and the professor started to speak, I often had the feeling: He is talking too much, he is disturbing me in my boredom. But afterward I would think very deeply about every single thing he had said, not that it interested me— it didn't interest me at all—but I relived everything. I relived it from the very beginning exactly the way it had been presented. Sometimes I went over it so thoroughly that it would actually take two hours. I would have two

hours of artificial boredom. In this process, one can make
an extraordinary discovery. This kind of discovery is one
that could be made at the end of the nineteenth century.
Imagine that you have come out of a lecture by a giant
rhinoceros of a man—this can happen!—and that you
have been bored to death.

Now, you can meditate, as I was saying, on this boring
lecture, bringing everything that was boring back into
yourself, into your soul. And suddenly, behind that giant
rhinoceros who was presenting you with all this boring
stuff, a higher person, something like a completely spiritual human being, will emerge. The whole lecture hall is
thereby transformed for you. I am putting this in a way
you can understand rationally. The lecture hall becomes
transformed in such a way that behind the professor, the
spiritual—a truly and deeply intelligent person—appears.
I knew many professors of the nineteenth century with
whom this was the case; but of course I don't want you to
talk about this, because people would think it a terrible
thing. For the truth is that humans are not inwardly as
unconscious or as unintelligent as they pretend to be.
Often they are quite smart. The most slow-witted are
often quite smart, and the opposite is also true. But they
don't know their own intelligence. It is a very deep secret:
behind people there stands the true nature of their soul
and spirit, which they often cannot perceive themselves.
This is already a way of reaching into the spiritual world.

As you know, at the end of the nineteenth century materialistic natural science became prominent, and people
today still adore this materialist science. I must admit
however, that this science was tremendously useful to me.
What it did, from start to finish, was bring up the most
boring statements. It is as if modern scientists lick their
fingers with enjoyment when they think they have proven

that all humans descended from apes. But if one thinks about this statement again and again, with complete energy, it changes! It changes into another statement that is spiritually correct. That is to say, humans do not descend from apes but from a spiritual being.

There are different points of view here. As when a young child was sent to school—too early as it turned out—and he heard for the first time from his teacher that humanity is descended from apes. When he returned home, he said to his father, "Hey, I heard today that humanity is descended from apes. Just think of that!" "Well," said his father indignantly, "You're certainly a stupid fellow. That may be the case for you, if you like, but not for me!" You see, for the father—he took it with reference to the soul—the story was quite unbelievable.

From all that I have told you, you will see that one can find one's way into natural scientific thinking in two ways. If you have not studied natural science, as many did in the nineteenth century and indeed still do, instead of simply parroting the conclusions, you can think about them—but think about them in a meditative way. Think them over for hours and hours, and you will find that what is true in the spiritual world comes forward. If you think for a long time about plants and minerals, and you have thought all the things about them that people tell you these days in a materialistic way, then you finally come to the meaning of things like the meaning of the zodiac, the meaning of the stars, all the secrets of the stars.

The surest way to this goal is to start with those simple statements that are taken for granted, and proceed forward from there: The part is greater than the whole; bodies have no extension; judgments have color; a straight line is the longest path between two points. With these kinds of statements you tear yourself away from your physical body. When you have experienced all this, you come to the point where you can use your etheric body instead of your physical body. You can then start thinking with your etheric body—your etheric body thinks everything upside-down, or in the reverse of the way it appears in the physical world. It is the etheric body that gradually brings one into the spiritual world. At precisely this point, however, one often gets stuck: one must accustom oneself to yet one thing more.

One sometimes reads very strange things these days. Once, in a small southern Austrian town (which is no longer in Austria), I was reading a so-called editorial in the evening paper. It was a very interesting story, in all details—every particular—a political story. There were three columns—it was all very interesting. Then at the end—still on the same page, there was a small disclaimer that said: We are sorry to notify our readers that everything in today's editorial article has been found to be based on false information, and therefore not a word of it is true! This is the kind of thing that can happen today. This of course is rather an extreme case, but whenever you read newspapers it can happen that on every single page there is something that is not true at all. What one reads today might very well be exposed at some later point as untrue. My feeling is that most people have become insensitive in such matters, and they take in, quite evenhandedly, both truth and lies. The mind has become blunted in this way, so that truth and lies are both taken in the same way. This makes it impossible to reach into the spiritual world.

I told you last time that when someone becomes mentally ill, only the body is sick; the soul is not sick, it remains healthy. I told you that when someone hallucinates in a fever, it is only the thoughts that become distorted—the soul itself is intact. One must get used to these things, if one wants to penetrate the spiritual world. One must get used to feeling pain in one's soul when something is not right, and to finding that something that is correct gives one spiritual joy. One must rejoice about truth the way one would if one were to receive a million dollars. One must be happy when one is told some truth. The opposite case is that when something is discovered to be a lie, a suffering is felt in the soul—not in the body—suffering as if one had a terrible illness. The suffering need not be so severe that the soul has to become sick, but it must be possible for the soul to experience pain and joy the way the physical body is moved to feel pain and joy. This means that one must come to the point where one feels the truth in the same way that one experiences happiness, cheerfulness, and general pleasure in the physical world. One must eventually come to the point where one suffers such pain in the face of untruth that one's soul becomes actually sick—as one can be in a bodily way. If someone heaps lies upon you, you must be able to say inwardly: Oh! this person has just given me deadly nightshade. This must be true in an inner way. Now of course, if you look at the current world—for instance, at the newspapers—one consumes deadly nightshade all the time. You must constantly nourish yourself spiritually, for the soul has to remain healthy. You must continually be spitting out what is bad, spiritually, if your spirit is to remain healthy. One has to get used to this fact, because one cannot be without newspapers. Once you experience the spiritual world, you will have to be used to the bad taste of newspapers; and to feeling joy when you read something exceptionally good—the same kind of joy, in my opinion, that you would have when you eat something that tastes very good.

Truth, and the striving for truth, must taste good to you; and lies, once you are conscious of them, must taste bitter and poisonous. You must not only know that judgments have color, but also that printer's ink nowadays is mostly wild cherry juice. You must be able to experience this in all honesty and rectitude, and once you can do so you will be in a state of spiritual transformation. People read these days about alchemy, and believe it in an external way. They believe that they can change copper to gold, and there are charlatans who will tell you all kinds of superstitious variations of this. Of course, in the spiritual world these things are possible; but one must believe in the truth of the spirit. One must be able to tell oneself that the printer's ink used is the same everywhere, materially, whether it has printed a true book or a lying newspaper. In the second case, the printer's ink is really wild cherry juice, and in the other it is like liquid gold. Things that in the physical world are exactly the same are quite different in the spiritual world. Of course, if intelligent people today hear you say that printer's ink can be liquid gold or wild cherry juice, they will tell you that you are only speaking "metaphorically." It is only a metaphor! But the metaphorical must become spiritual reality, and one needs to understand how metaphors becomes spiritual.

I will give you an example—it actually comes out of the history of the Social Democratic Party. You probably did not experience this as much in this country. At one point the party split; on one side were those led by [August] Bernstein—happily making all kinds of compromises with the middle class—and on the other side, led by [Eduard] Bebel, were the radicals.[5] I am sure you have heard about Bebel in books. At one point in Dresden there was a party convention, and Bebel got angry about the others and said he was going to put some order into Social Democracy.

He gave a big angry speech. In the course of it he said: "Well, if this or that happens on the other side, it feels like a louse running across my liver." Now everybody would say this is only meant metaphorically. Of course there is no such thing as a louse on his liver! But then one can ask: Why use such an expression? Why is it possible to speak in terms that suggest a louse walked on your liver?

For the most part, it is extremely unpleasant to have lice. There was, however, one sorry fellow who was unperturbed by it. He was always picking lice from his head. Someone asked him, "How is it that you are so skillful and always manage to find a louse?" He answered, as if he were quite lucky, "Its easy. If I miss the one I'm aiming for, I get the one beside it." It does not happen to all of us to aim for a louse and miss, and still get one!

When people have lice, it's terribly unpleasant—a distressing feeling. I remember a case when I was a tutor and one of the boys entrusted to me came home after being out. He had been sitting on all kinds of benches in a big city and he started to have dreadful pains in his eyes. Everyone was wondering which specialist to take him to for his terrible pains, but I suggested first trying a lice-killing cream on his eyebrows. Indeed, it was then noticed that he was full of lice, and once the cream went to work, his eyes stopped tearing. Now, you should have seen how upset people—the mother and the aunt—looked when they suddenly discovered that he had lice. Their feelings were so intense that they had repercussions in their livers; they had pains in their bellies. They said, "My God, our child has lice, what a terrible thing!" When this happened, the sensation was really as though they had lice running across their livers.

In the case of the Social Democratic Party, it was not a matter of people getting lice, but rather of some people doing things that seemed so awful, so repugnant to the others, that the sensation was the same—the same as would have been experienced in earlier times, or would still be experienced in some classes of society, at the thought of having lice on one's liver. So you can see, in the way the expression was formed, it did correspond to a reality. Latterly, however, these expressions have been used in a way that only refers to spiritual matters or matters of the soul. But again, one has consciously, deliberately, to make those connections. One must really be able to experience, not just the sound of the phrase, but the actual sensation that it came from.

Let us say I have a newspaper in front of me: most of the things that are printed in it must be felt by me as if the printer's ink was a toxic deadly nightshade juice. I wonder what people would do if they truly experienced that these days? Think for a moment how much deadly nightshade juice is used when, for instance, people talk about war guilt—Germany's war guilt in the First World War, or Germany's innocence in the war—and the fact that people, just by reason of belonging to this or that nation, feel comfortable when they claim innocence, using all manner of untruthful statements. They feel good doing this, but not because what they say is actually true.

So, how in today's world can one reach the spirit? One must, first of all, make a firm decision, a very intense commitment, to be very different from these contemporaries—and yet get along with them. For of course it is not going to be very helpful to just stand on a stage and insult people. One way or another, one has to find an avenue for truth. This is extremely difficult, as I have shown you today. Today I had to present difficult things so that you would see that it is not easy to enter the spiritual world. You will see that it is good to work with difficult things. Later on we will come to things that are easier, less strenuous. Next time, I will show you the whole way into the spiritual world.

3

Developing Honesty in Thinking

July 7, 1923

In the last lecture I told you that contemporary humanity cannot know anything because our thinking nowadays does not lead to real knowledge. In earlier times, say a thousand or fifteen hundred years ago, whoever wanted to learn anything had to undergo special training in thinking. People did not believe that they could understand anything of the spiritual world with their ordinary, everyday thinking, and therefore there existed a kind of schooling of thinking. Today, on the other hand, none of the education we receive enables us to educate our thinking in any real way.

This means that we are quite unable to think. I will give you an example that you probably saw in the newspaper a few days ago.[6] There was an article on a very common dream, a recurrent dream of flying. We can all remember dreams of flying, floating, or falling. Such dreams often occur soon after we go to bed. But you know all this. In this article a writer, versed only in today's natural scientific thinking, attempts to explain this kind of dream. You will see that this kind of thinking leads nowhere in such matters. According to Dr. Richard Traugott: "This dream of flying is actually induced or triggered by a contraction of the body." What is the writer saying here, what does he believe? He thinks that at the time of going to sleep the body contracts or twitches. But, I ask you, has it not happened to you that you have had this same experience when you are awake? And when does it happen to you? As far as what I have seen, this kind of sudden jolt or start happens when someone is afraid. It is when you experience something startling or frightening that you experience that kind of bodily jerking or contracting. The same thing can happen if, let's say, you go out onto the street and you see a man whom you believed to be in America. At the moment you notice him, your body is jolted— because you are surprised. Now you could not imagine that starting with what has just been described you would feel yourself flying! The problem is that people can invent all kinds of ideas, but those ideas do not particularly fit the observation. The thoughts seem to fit as long as one makes experiments in the laboratory with lifeless matter; but the minute one tries to explain something in real life, they don't fit anymore.

Let us continue with this writer. He says: "The cause of this contraction resides in the difference of muscle tension in sleeping and in waking. In the waking state there is a constant flow of energy from the central nervous system to the muscles." He assumes that in the waking state there are constant electric currents moving between the muscles and the nerves. "These energy currents create the muscle tension necessary for the maintenance of the bodily balance that the harmonious interplay of the musculature requires. In sleep this muscle tension largely disappears. During the period of going to sleep the reflexivity of the spinal cord actually increases, and thus the relaxation of the muscle tension, or rather the stimulus that this process exerts on the spinal cord, easily leads to this twitching reflex." So presumably, in the nervous system of the spinal cord there is a stimulus that is continuous and that increases the muscle tension. The writer goes on: "Other sensations that exist in our organs, particularly the rising and falling movements of the chest musculature and the rib cage, may even more directly influence the development of this feeling of flying, floating in the air, or swimming." In other words, muscle tension increases, contracting the body to such an extent that finally, when we are asleep, we experience a condition like that of flying or swimming.

Now, after all this, just think back in your own experience to when you were breathless (panting) and your chest was tight. Did it ever occur to you that you were having a swimming sensation—not to mention the sensation of flying? On the contrary, in such moments you feel particularly heavy. The article goes on to say other things. For instance, attention is called to the amount of pressure and resistance we feel, when awake, on our bodies where they rest on something. Then, supposedly, when we fall asleep, we become aware of the lack of pressure and resistance. But really, this doesn't make sense. After all, when we are awake and walk, we actually are supported only on a very small surface! We feel that we are walking on the soles of our feet. Of course, when we sit down, we are resting on a larger surface than the soles of our feet. But even if you were to add the surface area of both these places where the body contacts the outside world, this still does not compare to the surface we need when we are asleep. So, as you can see, this kind of thinking really leads one to talk nonsense. This kind of thinking is what passes for science today. Our same scientist tells us that the electric currents in the nerves are stronger when we are asleep; they stimulate the muscles, and they cause the sensation of flying—

so that one believes one is flying. Or he tells us that the support disappears when we sleep! One can hardly believe what he goes on to say, for he speaks of: "the disappearance of the perception of pressure and resistance, that in the waking state is present in all the parts of the body that need a support...." It is not to be believed that he could fail to take into account that there is a much larger surface being used in sleep. But he doesn't care about this, because contemporary thinking never really reaches any real explanations or clarifies what really happens when we go to sleep.

Let me now clarify what really happens when we go to sleep. From this you will see how one can really achieve insight into the higher, spiritual world. First I will show you this in an image. Remember that this is only an image! Let's assume you have here someone's physical body. [He draws it on the blackboard.] Within it, there is an etheric, supersensible body—I will draw it in yellow. This fills out the physical body and is invisible. When we are asleep, these two bodies remain behind in the bed.

When we are awake, the astral body is also within these two bodies—I will draw the astral body in red here. Within the astral body there is the "I," the fourth member—I will show it in violet. This, then, is the human being when awake: physical body, etheric body, astral body, and "I"—inserted one within the other.

Let us now look at our sleeper: when he is in bed, he has only a physical body and an etheric body. Outside these are his astral body and "I." What lies in the bed therefore may be compared to a plant, for the plant also has a physical body and an etheric body. If a plant had no etheric body it would be a stone, and it would not be alive and could not grow. So what is lying in bed is like a plant—the plant does not think, and what lies in bed does not think in the sense of conscious thought. But it is also true that thoughts are in there somewhere, as I have already explained to you; and sometimes these thoughts are even more clever than those we have when we are conscious. However, there are no daytime thoughts such as we are used to, and in this respect what lies in bed is like a plant.

What lives outside that which lies in bed can be described as feeling no boundaries. You can start to have an explanation of this, if you notice that when you leave the boundaries of your body, your consciousness disappears. When you are in your physical body, your astral body is constrained by it; but when you leave the physical body, then your astral body suddenly grows—it grows to gigantic dimensions, because the physical body no longer contains it and makes it small. At the moment you go to sleep, at the moment you move out of your physical body, you feel as if you were growing larger and larger.

Now, let's say you drink a glass of something. I guess I'd better not say a glass of alcohol, or else the word would be spread that I speak in favor of alcohol. As you know this is a rather unpleasant issue in Switzerland these days. So let us say you drink a glass of water with a little raspberry juice. If you put some raspberry juice in a glass of water, you can taste the raspberry juice easily. If, however, instead of a glass, you take a small bucket containing the equivalent of five bottles of water, and if you put only the same amount of raspberry juice in it as you put earlier in your glass, the raspberry juice is diluted—spread out over a much larger amount of water. You have much less of the raspberry taste. When I was a little boy, I grew up in the vicinity of a winery. There were big cellars with barrels of four hundred buckets of wine. If we had filled one of these with water instead of wine and had added a little raspberry juice and stirred it, you could have drunk the water without at all realizing there was raspberry juice present. This is clear, I am sure. Now, as long as the astral body is as small as the physical body it is like the raspberry juice in the glass of water; your astral body expands only to the limit of your physical body. But when you leave the physical body in sleep, it no longer contains the astral. The astral body spreads out, just as the raspberry juice spreads out in the four hundred buckets of water. Therefore, in your astral body you have no consciousness. Consciousness is created through the fact that the astral body is concentrated or contracted.

Here you have a true explanation for what actually happens when you go to sleep. As long as we are awake, our astral body is in our fingers and our toes, in all our muscles. When we feel the astral body in our muscles, we have the feeling of being dependent on our physical body. The physical body is heavy. We feel the heaviness of the physical body. In the moment we leave the physical body, we leave behind its heaviness. In this brief moment before consciousness has completely disappeared in sleep, we no longer feel the heaviness. We do not feel that we are falling, for in fact we are rising; we feel, rather, that we are floating into the air. This sense of not being bound to a physical body, this sense of enlargement, is what we experience as flying or swimming. We can feel ourselves moving freely until consciousness disappears and we go to sleep completely. In contrast to what has just been described, all the natural scientist can say is: our muscles twitch. And, as you well know, when our muscles twitch we feel them more than we usually do, and when that happens, it does not make us feel that we are flying—on the contrary, that is when we feel most closely tied to the physical. Another example is that when a man is surprised— Wow!—his mouth gapes open. This is because he is then so much connected with his muscles that he can no longer control them. The experiences of one's muscles twitching in surprise, or loosing control when "wowed," are the opposite of those prevailing when we go to sleep. When we go to sleep, we leave behind our muscles; therefore there cannot be a contraction of the muscles. When we lie down and rest on a larger surface of our bodies, there is rather a relaxation of the muscles. We do not need to hold our muscles together by means of our astral body. They relax, they do not become tenser. Because we no longer need to exert an influence on them, we believe that we are free of our muscles, and because of this we fly away with our lighter astral body.

Now consider for a moment what I told you last time about learning to think in a way opposite to our everyday thinking. Here you can see how today's ordinary thinking, when trying to explain the human being, results in the opposite of the truth. Therefore the first thing you must do is to think correctly—which really means being able to think the opposite of what holds true in the physical world.

People have lost the habit of thinking correctly. They can no longer think in such a way that they can reach the spiritual world through thinking.

There are many people today who speak our language, and this language contains the word "spirit," so they use it. The problem is that they no longer have any real picture of what the word "spirit" means. They can make mental pictures only of physical things. But if we want to think of the spiritual, we come to something without physical characteristics, and therefore to something that you cannot perceive in the physical world. But thinking today is so tainted that people actually wish to see the spiritual world in a physical way. As a result of this, they become what we call spiritists. They say to themselves: If a physical body can move a table, the fact that I can do this means I exist. Then, they will continue: If a spirit exists, it must also be able to move a table. And this is how the practice of "table-tapping" originated. People rely on table-tapping for signals from the spiritual world. This is because their thinking has become twisted or warped. Their thinking is materialistic in nature. It says: I must have the spiritual, but I must have it in a physical guise. Spiritism is the most materialistic concept of all, and it is very important to understand that.

Now perhaps someone will say: But I have been present where people sat around a table and linked hands in a chain, and the table started to move and hop around, and all kinds of things of that sort. The external facts are true. It is quite possible to sit around a table, to make a chain of hands, and at some point the table will be set in motion. But this is the case when any small motion in some way starts a larger motion. If we have a railroad train with a locomotive and an engineer, the driver does not get out of his engine and go to the back of the train and start pushing it when he wants to start moving. In fact, he would not be able to do that. He would never be able to set a train into fast motion in this way. As you well know, the engineer makes a very small motion, and the train soon starts to move very fast and pull many cars. Why? Because the connections are established in the right way so as to result in the train moving. In this way, physically, a very small motion starts a larger motion.

This is the case in the purely physical process of people creating a chain of hands around a table. They then start to twitch very slightly and, lo, and behold! from these small motions a larger motion results. This motion is transferred through the material plane. But this is really a very ordinary physical event.

Now, from any person among those present at the table-tapping who has subconscious thoughts—these thoughts can be translated into the twitching of the finger tips, causing a response, which forms letters that we then read. However, what we read as an answer in such cases was always present somewhere in the subconscious of one of the people there. This is true, no matter how clever the answers seem to be. I have explained to you that when people enter into their subconscious, they are entering something much more profound than their ordinary consciousness. This is can be seen in the practice of table-tapping. Nevertheless, the fact of people turning to spiritism is proof of the strength of materialism in our time.

Ordinary thinking does not bring us to any true explanation of what a human being is. That was obvious from the newspaper article I mentioned here today wherein there was an attempt simply to explain a flying dream. The author of the article explains it in exactly the opposite way to which it should be explained. People no longer seem able to study things of real interest. I have often talked to you about dreams. Let me now repeat a few important facts.

Let's say a man is dreaming that he is in a town square in Basel. Suddenly—in dreams everything is possible—he finds himself standing in front of a fence. The fence has pickets: here one, there another; and here one is missing and there is a gap; and then another picket, and another gap. Now he dreams that he wants to jump over the fence, and he impales himself on one of the pickets, and this hurts—hurts so much that he wakes up and notices that he has not been impaled, but rather that he has a terrible toothache. He has a toothache and it wakes him up. He has a missing tooth in his upper jaw and he also has another missing tooth and this is what he saw in his dream picture as missing pickets in a fence. There was an exact correspondence to his upper jaw and its missing teeth. He then touches one of his teeth and he finds out which one hurts him. There is a cavity, and it hurts. One can certainly have such a dream.

What is really happening here? This whole episode was actually played out in the dreamer's waking life. You can really say: So long as I was asleep, I was happy; I did not feel my awful toothache. Why not? It is because the astral body was outside the physical body, and the etheric body does not feel the toothache. You can hit a stone as much as you want, and even break little pieces off it, but the stone as such does not feel it. You can tear a plant and the plant will not feel it, because it does not have an astral body—it has only an etheric body. You would soon stop picking roses and other flowers in the meadows, if the plants were to hiss like snakes because it hurt them. However, it does not hurt the plant, and a human being, when asleep, is like a plant. As long as we are asleep, the tooth does not hurt. But when the astral body slips back into the physical body, as soon as this happens, we 'inhabit' our teeth. Then, you see, the astral body is in the teeth. Only when we are completely in our body do we feel what hurts our body. When we are not quite within our body, what hurts appears to us as an external object.

Say, for instance, I burn a match: when looked at from without I will see it burning white. But if I had somehow lived within that match with my conscious astral body, I would not have only seen it externally. I would have felt it as a pain! In the case of the teeth, until I am fully in my body, when I first slip in, I feel them as if they were external objects, and I therefore make an external picture of them for myself that in some way resembles some aspect of them. Since I cannot make quite the right picture, which I could do only through spiritual science, I make a picture of a row of pickets instead of a row of teeth. Where there are gaps in my row of teeth, I have gaps in the row of pickets. As you can see, as a result of the confused picture that arises as a consequence of not quite being fully in the body, there is an error. Because when we are asleep we are outside our bodies, the inner is interpreted as the outer. I have been able to study what happens in such cases when observing little children as I taught them. They have no feeling as yet for the correct use of speech and I have often experienced that a child who has just started to write "Zahn," the word for tooth, will instead write "Zaun," the German word for fence. Such a child has to be told that this is false, wrong. Somehow the child was scared entering his body—not leaving it, but entering it. This does not cause a flying dream but a fearful dream, a nightmare. The child has a nightmare and somehow expresses this in the form of the fence dream. There is a connection between the child's misuse of words and the images of the dream. The images of the dream come into existence through words. There are always verbal connections. These help us to see more clearly what is really happening.

The man I referred to before—Richard Traugott—has written a great deal about dreams, most of it is as absurd as what he wrote about the flying dream.[7] When he speaks, equipped with ordinary science, he says exactly the opposite of what is actually the case. He does not understand that because the astral body grows larger when leaving the physical body it perceives itself as flying, and that when it is forced to shrink on reentering it pictures itself as someone (or something) who is squeezed somehow. The muscles tighten, causing an anxiety dream. The anxiety dream occurs precisely when the man who wrote the article would claim that there should be a flying dream. It is also possible to have anxiety dreams when the process of going to sleep does not proceed properly. Let's say, for example, that you are lying down and you have the sensation that you are being strangled by someone. This can happen if you are in the process of going to sleep and somewhere there is a disturbance, so that you cannot go to sleep, but you keep trying to do so anyway. You pass in and out of sleep, and returning into your body correctly is not quite possible because you are still tired. This can be felt as a strangling sensation, because the astral body is being forced in some way, and cannot quite enter correctly. Knowing this kind of thing, you can explain all these matters much better.

This brings us to the fact that one more thing is necessary if we really want to know the spiritual world. One must be absolutely clear about the fact that the physical body is not involved here. One must be able to live in the astral body alone, in a way that does not involve the physical body at all. If one wants to know the spiritual world, one must induce a sleeplike condition in oneself. In ordinary life this occurs only when one slips out of one's physical body, which is viewed externally as the condition of sleep. But as I mentioned in my example of the raspberry juice in the large casks of water, in sleep the astral body (or juice) normally becomes gigantic and this must not be allowed to happen. The astral body must be held together through an inner effort of another body. Do not think now about the astral body and the human "I," just think again about the image of the drops of raspberry juice. Create a vivid image of a glass of water with only one drop of juice in it. The raspberry juice expands in the water to the limit of the glass, but it is still perceptible. But then if you assume a container a hundred thousand times larger, then you would not be able to perceive anything of the juice, and this is comparable to our normal inner experience in sleep. Now, imagine for a moment that this drop of raspberry juice takes on an impish character. I put this impish drop in a cask with four hundred buckets of water; it has a real temper and says to itself: I am not going to let myself get mixed up in all this water, I am going to remain myself. Were this to happen, you would then have a huge casket with one drop of raspberry juice in it; and if you reached this drop with the tip of your tongue, if you went through all that water to the exact spot where the raspberry juice held itself together, then you would actually taste the sweetness of that single drop.

I must stress here that I am speaking only metaphorically about the raspberry juice with its impish character. The opponents of Anthroposophy can be quite funny at times. There was once an article in a Hamburg newspaper in which Anthroposophy was insulted from all possible sides; and there, it is true, I was actually seen as an imp or devil, and in that case indeed it was meant very seriously, as if I myself were not just an imp but the devil's own helper—as if I were the very devil come into the world. To return therefore to the image I gave you: the drop of raspberry juice is only a devil's imp insofar as it can keep itself quite small when it is put into the water.

In the case of the astral body, it is possible for it to stay as small when it leaves the physical body as it is when it is within the physical body; but it can develop the forces necessary to do this only by learning to think sharp, well-honed thoughts. I told you we must develop independent thinking. This independent thinking is much stronger than the weak thinking of most people.

The first requirement for knowledge of the spiritual world is very sharp and well-honed thinking. The second requirement is the ability to think backward. The outer physical world proceeds forward, therefore one needs to learn to think in reverse. This strengthens one's thinking. One must learn that truth which I told you about last time: the part is greater than the whole. This once again is something that contradicts what the physical world seems to indicate; but if one can do this one can put oneself into the spiritual world. All these things I have mentioned cause the astral body to remain small in spite of the fact it is not contained in the physical body—so that it does not simply flow out into the common astral ocean.

All these requirements fit together, but you must be careful that all these things are taken with the same sobriety and the same scientific attitude with which the physical world is ordinarily examined. The moment we slip into fantasy, we are finished with the scientific. Our clear and definite approach must never be allowed to turn into fantasy.

Let's take the case when one has a pain in one's big toe. You feel this pain through your astral body. If we had only a physical body, we would not feel the pain; and likewise if we had only an etheric body, we would not feel the pain. If this were not true, a plant would squeal when it was plucked! We cry out when we have a pain in our big toe— of course, we don't actually squeal, but you know what I mean. We all feel like crying out when we experience a pain of this kind. Why is this?

Our astral body is spread throughout our whole physical body, and when our astral body reaches the spot where something in our big toe is out of order, this is brought up to the brain by the astral body, and we have a mental picture of our pain. But let's assume someone has a sick brain that does not allow him to register the pain in his big toe in that certain spot in the brain where it is normally felt. One

needs a healthy place in one's brain to be able to register
the pain in one's big toe. Assuming this spot in the brain is
sick, and remembering what I have told you—that neither
the soul nor the astral body can become sick—the pain in
your big toe cannot be registered. What happens under
these conditions? The specific place in the individual's
physical brain is sick, but this still leaves the etheric aspect
of the brain. The etheric aspect of the brain that remains is
not properly supported by the physical part, and we may
therefore ask: What will the etheric body do in such a
case? The etheric body makes a great deal of this toe; not
only does it notice it, it makes a mountain of it. The pain
to the etheric body will appear to us as little beings, little
mountain-climbing beings sitting in this mountain. So here
we have the big toe transferred into a spatial picture, into a
large space—just because the brain is ill. If this were to
happen to you, you would swear that there was a mountain in front of you. In actuality this mountain is only your
big toe, and it is clear that this is a delusion.

It is very important to protect oneself from such delusions when one penetrates into the spiritual world, or else
one can slip into total fantasy. How can we avoid these
delusions? This has to be done through real schooling. We
must learn what can result when the physical body
becomes sick in any way, so that we will not be confused
when merely physical manifestations appear to be real
spiritual occurrences! For this reason we must learn truly
active thinking, thinking backwards, thinking such as I
described before—a thinking very different from our ordinary thinking in the physical world. In this way one will
be protected against delusion, and one will recognize the
physical origin of what we have just described. In earlier
times, there was a real method or art of preparation,
called dialectic, that trained people to penetrate safely into

the spiritual world.. This meant that people really had to learn to think. Nowadays, if one were to suggest to people that they must first learn to think, they would pull our hair out—for everyone is convinced that they already know how to think. But if one looks back to earlier times, it is actually true that there was a real schooling of thinking, or a dialectic. One had to be able to think both forward and backward, and one had to be able to form concepts in the right way.

How, we might ask, did this training take place? It took place through the activity of speaking, and at the same time as one spoke, one learned to think. I have just given you an example of this, when I talked of children first learning to speak and then learning to think. But of course such thinking is at first entirely childlike. Nowadays this childlike thinking is preserved by people throughout life, although it is worthless in later life. If one were to continue to learn thinking through speaking this way, then one would have to ensure that with each inbreath and each outbreath the air moved correctly in and out; for correct speaking is connected with correct breathing. For speaking to be rightly connected to the breathing process the air must come in and go out in the proper manner.

Much depends on one's being prepared for correct speaking, because correct speaking prepares one for correct breathing. Whoever knows how to breathe correctly can also speak for a long time without becoming tired. Through the art of dialectic, one once learned how to speak and breathe correctly, and therefore how to think properly. These days, however, people are no longer able to think properly, for their breath keeps bumping into the organ of their breathing at every moment. Just listen to some academics when they speak. First of all, they do not speak very much in general; they usually read, and they use their eyes very much for support. But if you listen to academics speaking, for the most part it is as if they were short of breath. It is as if they were constantly bumping into their own body.

For this reason everything that is said becomes a picture of the physical body. It is all the same, whether one has a sick spot in one's brain and consequently makes a mountain—with mountain spirits—out of a painful big toe, or whether one keeps bumping into oneself with one's breath whenever one thinks, with the result that true thinking cannot emerge. Because your breath is constantly bumping into your physical body, you will perceive the whole world as a physical phenomenon. Now, what really is the source of this materialism? Materialism comes from two facts: people do not know how to think correctly, and they do not breathe out correctly. It seems to them as if the whole world were made up of pressure and thrust—which they have in themselves—because they have not been prepared through right thinking. Therefore we can say: A man is a materialist because he cannot get out of himself; inwardly, he keeps bumping into himself.

Let us return for a moment to Mr. Traugott. What he should really say is that the flying dream is caused by the fact that we go out of ourselves, and the astral body starts to grow larger. However, he does not conclude this. He thinks, indeed he thinks a great deal. And what happens if someone wants to think, and think some more, when in fact he is unable to think? What really happens? First of all, you will see him frown, and if this doesn't help he will hit his forehead and thus tighten his muscles, and then he tightens them some more, and he may even hit himself again so that his muscles are really tight. What is Mr. Traugott really doing when he is thinking about dreams. Instead of looking at things as they really are, he tightens his own muscles, and what he finds is what he himself is doing—muscle tension. "I've got it," he says, "the dream is caused by muscle tension!" He confuses his own attempt at thinking about dreams with reality. We can all learn something from Mr. Traugott. We can learn what is happening to him when he thinks about things, and when you yourself read the story. What happens today when we read what people print is that we learn what they themselves imagine is true. Whenever we read the newspapers today, we have to say we really learn very little about what is really happening in the world, but we do learn what the people who sit in the editorial rooms would like to be happening in the world.

The same is true of today's materialistic science. Through it you will not learn what the world is; rather, you will learn what materialist professors think about the world. If you penetrate this a little, you will see that Anthroposophy has no intention of deceiving the world, but in fact it wants to put honesty in the place of deception and illusion, and in place of what is often untrue, very often consciously so.

You may see from this discussion that honesty, inner honesty, is the fourth quality that must be present if we are to be able to reach into the spiritual world. If you contemplate the world in this way, you will see there is very little honesty operating in the world, and it is no surprise that not much of it can be seen in science.

We have therefore seen four required qualities: independent thinking, thinking not linked to the outer world, thinking whose quality is completely different from the physical world, and thinking honestly. We will look at other characteristics next time.

4

Learning to Live Correctly in the Outer World

July 18, 1923

There are many questions still pending from those asked recently, but I will tie in some of these with the recent subject of dreams. I shall start with a question that seems to have broken many scholars' heads, and that is the question of the lizard's tail.

As you may know, when one of these large lizards is grabbed by the tail, the tail breaks. In fact, it is very difficult to catch such lizards because when the tail breaks, the lizard runs away quite happily without its tail. The tail seems brittle, and scientists attempt to establish whether the tail is really torn away or if it is somehow left behind by the animal. Contemporary science proceeds in a materialistic way and therefore tends to assume that the animal simply has weak muscles there and that these muscles just cannot hold together under the strain of being caught. But there is an undervalued fact, one which is often not even noticed, that when the lizard is caught and kept in captivity for a long time it loses the ability to let go of its tail. It is as if the tail becomes stronger and stronger, and therefore increasingly difficult to pull off. The peculiar thing is that when the lizard is in the wild it lets go of its tail easily, and when it is in captivity the lizard holds onto it.

What is really going on here?

You see, people direct their thoughts toward the musculature around the tail, instead of looking at all the facts, facts that would very easily give the answer to why the lizard in captivity does not lose its tail. The missing evidence is that the animal in the wild is frightened when one tries to catch it. The first time a human comes into its vicinity the lizard is scared and it becomes so brittle that it will let go of its tail when you grab it. Once the lizard becomes used to the proximity of people—when people are constantly near it—the lizard loses its fear and likewise stops losing its tail.

Even a superficial observation of all the facts in this situation leads us to conclude that fear plays a very important role in the case of the lizard. But we must examine this fear more carefully and say: The fear that this lizard has when people come near it to catch it—this somehow comes out of the animal when it is caught, though normally it remains inside. It is this fear that holds the matter in the tail together and makes it strong!

Let me introduce here a remarkable phenomenon of human life. When people who are very dependent on their soul life become scared they get diarrhea. The fear causes diarrhea. How can we understand the meaning of this? This means that whatever is normally held in their intestines is no longer held together as it was. When fear rises up in the soul it stops holding things together in the intestines, but when fear remains in the intestines it holds things together.

The same thing is true of the lizard. If one looks at a lizard, it is like one's own lower body: it is completely filled throughout with the soul quality of fear.

It is especially true of the tail that it is completely filled with fear; and when this fear is pressed out or expressed, the tail breaks. The fear, however, normally remains within the animal. The animal does not feel the fear while in captivity because it is used to people, and because of this the fear can remain in the tail and hold it together. Here we see a very important quality of soul that has a certain significance for the bodily constitution.

Human beings also contain fear. We have fear in our big toe, in our legs, in our belly—there is fear everywhere. This is not everywhere the case however. Fear does not normally rise above the diaphragm—it does so only when we have nightmares. Nevertheless, fear does have a role to play: it holds our organism together. It is in our bones that fear lives most strongly. The bones are strong and hard because a terrible fear lives in them. It is fear that holds the bones together. When we feel our bones too much, our bones get soft. Those children who were fearful at the time when their bones were not yet completely hardened, develop weak bones—a condition called rickets. It is possible to cure children of rickets by reducing their fear through some soul work. But it would be quite false to say that this fear in us is something of the soul: that we need only approach the fear in a somewhat higher manner in order to have an experience of a higher kind of knowledge. To enter this subject in the wrong way would not be good, for we would make ourselves sick in body and soul at the same time. We must do something entirely different.

In order to gain knowledge of the spiritual world—I have already given you various other means—we must learn to live correctly in the outer world. How do people really live in the outer world these days? As we said recently, we freeze terribly, and often we sweat a lot, and this is how most people normally experience living in the world. First they sweat, then they freeze. This is not the only way one can live into the outer world, however.

Rather one should try to cultivate a certain capacity, so that when it is cold one isn't just cold but rather one becomes aware of a kind of qualitative experience that goes with it, namely that of fear. When one is aware of fear, one easily notices that with the return of warmth fear disappears. When a person cultivates a certain awareness of fear connected with the coming of snow; when the warm rays of the sun bring a certain pleasant comforting feeling—that person is in fact living into the outer world in a way that leads to higher knowledge. This belongs with the other requirements I have tried to describe to you. It is really true that whoever wants to gain higher knowledge must feel something when he comes close to a glowing piece of iron, and he must feel something different when he approaches a piece of flint. When he approaches the glowing iron, the feeling should arise: here is something that is related to my own warmth and is good. But when he picks up a piece of flint he should feel a sense of strangeness and a somewhat fearful mood. (You can see immediately that whoever wants to gain higher knowledge cannot be nervous, as we say these days, or else he would drop the piece of flint the minute he takes it into his hand, because he is afraid of it!) One must be brave and conquer the fear. At the same time we cannot be like a moth that takes so much pleasure in the light that it flies right into it, to its death.

The example of the insect flying into the flame gives you a good idea of the relationship of a flame to the spiritual world. We really must acquire a sensitivity to the inner feeling for whatever is at hand out there in nature. What will this produce? Let us examine things as they are now. Materialists assert above all that the earth has a crust of hard stone—they believe in this hard rock of the earth because they can walk on it and when they touch it, it is hard. Materialists believe in this hard rock, but whoever wants to gain higher knowledge should experience a certain fearfulness of this same hard rock. This fear is totally absent when a man finds himself in the warm air. I will draw the warmed air above the hard rock. [He draws on the blackboard.]

When one considers the warm air, fear is totally absent. (To show the warmth of the air I will color it red.) Yet it is possible to enter a condition such that even the warm air would make one afraid. This is the case when one attempts to get closer and closer to the feeling that one gets from the warm air. In a person who feels more and more comfortable living in the quality of the warm air, the warmth too will eventually cause fear. It seems strange, but the better one feels, the more fearful one becomes! When one gets used to feeling completely at ease in warmed air, when one becomes more and more used to the warmth and is fully at ease inside all of nature, then one can find spiritual knowledge. At this point something quite remarkable happens—I will try to make it clearer for you. Most people try to keep cool, to cool off when they get warm—all they know is that it is very pleasant to get cooled off. But if, instead of this, one were to remain warm, if one were to soak up the good feeling of the warmth, then what is in the warmed air (which I have drawn here schematically in yellow) would start to fill itself with all kinds of images, and the spiritual world would literally arise: the spiritual world, which is contained in the air, which one does not normally feel, and is not conscious of, because in most cases one cannot tolerate the warmth in the air. When one becomes accustomed to seeing those beings in the air, one gradually reaches the point where one can tell oneself: When I take a stone in my hand, it is very hard; but when

I become more and more aware of the spiritual, when I am able to penetrate into the spiritual, when there is more and more activity around me—not just the sensory world but also the spiritual world—I can do something more. I cannot slip into the hard ground with my physical body of flesh and blood, but with my astral body I can actually slip into the earth. This is very interesting—at the moment that one starts to perceive the spiritual world in the realm of the air, at that moment one slips so far out of one's body that stones are no longer perceived as obstacles—and one can actually dive into the hard earth the way a swimmer dives into water. What is interesting is that we cannot penetrate into the air as spirits, for there are already other spirits there, but in the earth, which is empty of spirit, it is very easy to gain entrance—one can dive under as a swimmer does.

In between solid and gaseous elements we have the watery element. This rises and falls as rain. Up above, as I am sure you have seen, there are sometimes formations of lightning. Water is between the hard earth and the air; it is thinner than earth and denser than air. What is the meaning here? This is something that is easiest to understand if we consider lightning.

So, according to the scientists, lightning is an electric spark. Let us examine why, according to them, it is an electric spark. You probably already know this but I will repeat it. If we take a sealing-wax rod and we rub it with a leather strap, it becomes electric; and if we have little pieces of paper, they are attracted by the rod; and so it is possible to electrify all kinds of objects by rubbing them. This is often shown to children in school. But there is also the specific need for something else. If you do this experiment in a very humid room, you will not be able to electrify a rod or anything else. First you must dry everything thoroughly with a dry cloth; then, and only then, can you produce some electricity, because water does not produce electricity.

Now, according to the scientists there are clouds up above that rub against each other and somehow produce electric sparks. Even the child can tell you that in order to produce electricity you must remove all water, for if there is anything wet in the apparatus you will not be able to produce any electricity—even a child can tell you this. This is the kind of nonsense we are being told: it is clearly impossible to produce lightning by clouds rubbing against one another.

Think for a moment whither the water evaporates—it rises and reaches higher and higher into the region of the spiritual; it moves away from matter empty of spirits here below and rises into the spiritual world above. It is actually spirit that produces what looks like our electric spark. For, as we rise, we move higher and higher into the regions of the spiritual. Matter is present only in proximity to the earth. Higher up, it is surrounded by the spirit. Therefore, at the moment when the water vapor rises and reaches the region of the spiritual, the flash is produced. The water first becomes more spiritualized and then it falls down again, "densified."

If one observes nature correctly, one is forced to come to spiritual subjects; but if one absolutely refuses to take the spiritual into consideration, one is then left with no alternative but to make all kinds of absurd statements like the ones you heard about the flying dreams or the lizard's tail or the cause of lightning. Everywhere we can look, it is clear that it is impossible to explain nature if one does not bring in the spiritual.

We will now proceed further. When one stands on the earth, starting from the feet and moving up, one is always related to the lower spiritual beings, and one can dive in like a swimmer. When we move out of our physical body with our astral body, we can actually penetrate into our solid surroundings and find ourselves within solid matter. (We cannot however do this with the surrounding air.) We can actually wander around, but this wandering around in the solid element has very important aspects. When we conduct ourselves correctly in relation to warmth then we come to the point of seeing spiritual beings in the air. But when we go out of our body at night and unite ourselves with the earthly in a spiritual form, then it can happen, when we awake, that we can still sense something around us of what we experienced when we were in the hard matter of the earth. Something remains in the soul.

Some of you may have noticed on awakening that it is easy to hear very soft sounds; and if, as you wake, you are really attentive you may have an experience similar to hearing someone knocking at the door. It is quite remarkable that when we live into the air with our soul there arise images, and when we live into the solid earth—into matter—with our soul, as a swimmer does who dives into water, then we experience tones.

It is very important to know that all hard matter continuously produces sounds that of course we cannot hear if we are not inside of it. All solid matter continuously contains tones and we can hear them on waking up only because we are still half in our surroundings. These sounds can have a very special meaning in certain cases. It is completely true, for example, that it sometimes happens, when a person dies at some distance, that someone else may hear on waking what sounds like a knocking at the door. This knocking sound is related to the person who died.

Now of course it is very difficult for one to understand these things properly. But just think: You would all be unable to read, that is, to make sense of signs or letters on paper, if you had not first learned to read. In the same way one cannot immediately understand the wonders at work when one hears tones on waking up. You do not of course have to believe that there is actually a dead person standing at the door knocking with his fingers. But the dead do reside on earth in the first days after death, and they do live in the solid material of the earth. The fact that tones arise in connection with solid bodies does not necessarily have to seem very remarkable. It was quite widely known in the past when people paid attention to such things. People can have a premonition when someone at a distance dies. This means that someone has died and is still bound in his soul to the solid earth. Tones arise out of the dead when they abandon the earthly realm. It is just as easy to hear the sounds that are made at a distance as it is to read a telegraph message from someone who has transmitted from America. These kinds of long distance effects transmitted through matter are present on earth and are always there, and in days when people paid attention to these things the connection of the spiritual with the earthly was well known. This is not some fairy tale; it is actually something that was perceived in earlier times.

We are now entering an area that is described nowadays as superstition. But it is actually possible to explain these things scientifically, just as other scientific things are explained; only you must know how to do this accurately.

One could come to the point of perceiving the spiritual world in the air: that is, if people were not so "poor me" as they so often are today. (The more civilized people become, the more depressed and plaintive they become in a certain way.) Those whose daily work forces them to live in great heat have no time during work hours to perceive the spiritual world and so they lose the opportunity to perceive the spiritual world contained in the air. The fact that one can see spiritual beings in the air is not in itself a dangerous thing; everybody could perceive those beings without further delay and without it in any way being dangerous.

However, in the case of hearing, if that seizes a person too strongly, and one enters a condition where one hears all kinds of things—that is a danger. The reason is that there are people who can come gradually to the point where they hear all kinds of things—they hear all kinds of things told to them. Such people are on the road to madness. There is a simple reason why there is never a danger in seeing the spiritual beings that are in the air. I will make it clear by using a comparison. If you were in a boat and you fell into the water you could drown; but then, if someone pulled you up, you could have all kinds of experiences, except that of drowning: you would not actually drown. In the same way, if the human soul goes out and up it can see all kinds of things; however if it sinks into solid matter, it does in a way drown spiritually. This spiritual drowning happens when people lose their own consciousness in that they give it up to all kinds of things that are told to them inwardly. It is not a very serious danger when a man sees the spiritual outwardly. This is the same as walking around in the world, and just as a man is not afraid of a chair that is in front of him, so gradually he stops being afraid of spiritual beings and actually enjoys what he sees. But when things are heard inwardly, then we sink into the solid earth with our whole spiritual life, with our whole soul life, and it is possible to drown in that— one stops being truly human. Therefore one must always look with some caution and wakefulness at those people who say that all kinds of things have been told to them inwardly. That is always dangerous. Only the human being who is firmly rooted in the spiritual world and knows his way about can understand what is really being said, which amounts to this: it can never be higher beings speaking in a case like this; it can only be spiritual beings of a lower nature.

I have told you these things in great detail so that you can see that as human beings we must come to a completely different conception of the outer world if we want to penetrate into the spiritual world. Of course there are people who can say: Why have the spirits made it so difficult for us to get to know them? But gentlemen, just think what kind of being a human would be if one didn't really have to make an effort to penetrate to the spiritual world—if one was always within it. One would be a purely spiritual automaton. A human being only comes to a proper relationship to the spiritual world, to the degree that he or she has really worked at it. It does indeed take the hardest inner effort in order to research and explore the spiritual world. It is not difficult to take one's ease at a laboratory bench and to make all kinds of experiments. It is quite easy to cut up corpses and thereby learn all manner of things; but it takes inner work to really penetrate into the spiritual world, and for this kind of work the contemporary, educated world is too lazy. Because of this laziness people say: I have made these exercises on how to reach knowledge of the higher worlds—but I didn't see anything. The problem is that such people believe that these things have to be given to them outwardly, not that they have to work and conquer them inwardly. This indeed is in keeping with what people nowadays want— they want everything to be ready-made for them. As I have mentioned to you already, human beings these days want to put everything on film. They want to make a film of everything so that they can look at everything from the outside.

If we want to make progress—real progress, spiritually—we must make sure that no matter what we take up from the world, we will work it through. Therefore, in the future, those people will penetrate most deeply into the spiritual world who will as much as possible avoid having everything on film for their comfort. Rather they should choose to think everything through for themselves, to think along, so that when people tell them things about the world they will be participants in the thinking. As you can see, I have not shown you a film! Even if we had time for it, I would not attempt to present things to you with a film. I have done a few drawings, but these were done at the time and you could see them being made, so you could see what I was trying to do with every stroke and were able to think along with me.

This is also what needs to be introduced in the education of children. Few finished drawings or pictures should be given, and as many as possible that are done in an impromptu manner. In this way the children work inwardly with the teacher. They become awakened to an inwardness that leads to a deeper living into the spiritual and thus enhance their understanding of the spiritual. Also one should not give children finished theories; this makes them dogmatic. What really matters in all cases is that they are brought into autonomous activity; this in turn will allow the whole body to be free.

I want to mention one other subject that arises from the questions I received from you. Many of you have read that potatoes were introduced into Europe at a particular time in history, for the people of Europe were not always potato-eaters. In fact a rather interesting story is related to this. There is something comical in an encyclopedia in which I myself collaborated—but not in the article in question. According to the article, it is universally agreed that Drake introduced the potato into Europe. In Offenburg, which is now occupied by the French, there is a monument to Drake. I looked it up in a conversational dictionary, and there it stood: The monument was erected to Drake in Offenburg, for it is rumored (wrongly) that he brought potatoes to Europe. One can say if anything is even attributed to a person, people in Europe will build a monument to him. But this is not what I wanted to talk about; rather, that at a particular time potatoes were introduced.

Let us now take a closer look at potatoes. When we eat potatoes we are not really eating a root; the roots are the little things dangling off the potatoes, and these are removed along with the peel when one cleans them. The potato itself is actually a thickened stem. An ordinary plant grows and it has a root and then a stem—and if the stem becomes thicker, as is the case with the potato, there arises a kind of knot or tuber, which is really a thickened stem. You should remember this when you are eating a potato— you are eating a thickened stem. We should ask, what does it mean for us that with the introduction of the potato into Europe we learned to like the taste of thickened stems?

If you look at a whole plant, it is made up of root, stem, leaves, and flower. [He draws this on the blackboard.] A plant is something quite remarkable. The roots down there become very similar to the soil insofar as they contain many salts; and the flower up here is very similar to the warm air, so that it is as if through the heat of the sun the flower were continuously cooked. As a result the flower contains many oils and fats. In other words, when we look at the plant we find roots at the bottom, and the root is rich in salts, whereas the flower is rich in oils. Therefore when we eat roots we introduce many salts into our intestines; these salts in turn make their way to the brain and stimulate it. If for instance someone suffers not from migraine headaches but from ordinary headaches—the type that seem to fill your head—it is very good for that person to eat roots. One can see how a certain salty sharpness is present in those roots, and this can already be established by the taste. If you eat a flower, the plant is in fact already half-cooked; the oils are already on the outside and this is what primarily fattens the stomach and the intestines and, in turn, affects the lower body. These are the kinds of things doctors have to take into account when they prescribe teas. There will never be a very strong influence on the head if someone cooks flowers in the tea; on the other hand, if you cook the roots, they will have a strong effect on the sick person's head.

So you can see that when considering the human being we pass from the stomach to the head or from the bottom to the top. With plants, we must do the opposite. To find the correspondence, we must proceed from the flower to the root. Remember—this may enlighten you as to the meaning of potatoes—that the root is connected with the head. The potato has a tuber, which is something that is not entirely turned into a root. Thus when you eat potatoes you are eating, by preference, plants that have not quite become roots. If one limits one's self to the eating of potatoes—too many potatoes—it is not possible to pay a proper amount of attention to the brain, so that all these potatoes stay down below in the digestive tract.

This is why we say that potato-eaters neglect their heads or brains. You will only perceive this connection if you are an adept of spiritual science. But one can say that ever since the habit of eating potatoes has become firmly established, the head has become less capable, and it is the tongue and throat that have been particularly stimulated.

This is why the potato is particularly appreciated as a side dish for people, because it stimulates the body below the head, leaving the head itself unburdened.

If, on the other hand, we eat red beets, we develop a great craving for the activity of thinking. This happens unconsciously. Potatoes only make one crave the next meal. Potatoes make one hungry because they don't quite reach the head. In contrast to this, the red beet satisfies so quickly because it actually reaches all the way to the head, and that is the most important thing. Of course it is very unpleasant for people to disturb their ease with thinking. Therefore they will very often eat potatoes more readily than red beets just for this reason: that to do so does not stimulate their thinking. They become lazy and their thinking becomes lazy. The red beet on the other hand stimulates thinking—it is a true root—insofar as it actually makes one want to think, and anyone who does not want to think does not like red beets. If you need to have your thinking stimulated, the salty stimulation of radishes, for instance, might be necessary. Anyone who is not quick in the head will get good results eating radishes—because the addition of radishes to his meals will set his thoughts into movement.

So we can now see a remarkable thing: the radishes stimulate thinking, and it is not necessary to be really active oneself; thoughts come naturally as a result of eating radishes; thoughts so strong that they also stimulate very powerful dreams. On the other hand, a man who eats a lot of potatoes will not have strong thoughts, and his dreams will make him heavier. If you habitually eat potatoes, you will find yourself constantly tired and always wanting to sleep and dream. You can see that there is enormous cultural and historical meaning in what foods people actually have access to.

One could say from what I have shown you: The way things really are we live completely in matter, from matter, and yet this is not true. I have often told you that human beings have a totally new body every seven years; it is constantly being renewed. Whatever matter was in our body eight to ten years ago is nowhere to be found now: it has been expelled. We have cut it away in the form of our nails and with our hair; it has run out of us with our sweat—it all goes out. Some of it goes out more quickly and some more slowly, but eventually it all passes out. So what is the true story? Well, this is more or less the way it goes. I will start by giving you a schematic drawing. Let us say this is the human being, who is constantly producing tissue, and expelling it, and always absorbing new matter; and of course it is easy to think: Well, it comes in through the mouth and it goes out in feces and urine. In this way the human body is seen as a kind of tube. The matter enters while we are eating, and then is expelled after we have held onto it for awhile: this is more or less the way digestion is presently thought of. But in the real human being nothing at all of earthly matter naturally goes in— this is an illusion. What really happens is the following: Let's say we eat potatoes. This does not mean that we actually absorb anything from the potatoes. Something in the potatoes stimulates us, it stimulates our throat, it stimulates our larynx, and so on—everywhere the potatoes go to work—and the result of this is that we receive the strength to expel the potatoes again. In this process of expulsion, something from the earth comes into us, but it comes from the ether, not from solid matter, and it is this that builds us up in the course of the seven years. We are really not built up from earthly matter. When we eat, we do so in order that we may be stimulated. In reality we are built from what is above us, so that all the ideas and conceptions people have of food coming in and food going out again, with the side effect of leaving some material inside, do not at all fit the situation. To repeat: what is really happening is that a stimulation occurs and in response to this stimulation a counter-force enters from the ether, and our whole body is built up from the ether. Nothing that we have in us is built from earthly matter. It is like this: when we push at something and there is a counter-push and a kind of reflexive push coming back to us, we must not confuse the pushing with the reflex action. We must not be confused by the fact we need food. The actual purpose of food is that we do not become lazy in the reconstitution of our bodies. We must not confuse this stimulating activity with the fact we happen to be taking in material food.

Now of course there can be all kinds of irregularities that enter the normal situation—such as, if we eat too much, the food stays in us too long, and we accumulate matter that should not be there—fat. And if we take in too little, then we are not stimulated enough and we absorb too little of what we need from the spiritual world, from the etheric world, which is so necessary; for we do not build ourselves from the earth and its matter but rather we actually build ourselves up from what is outside the earth.

If it is the case that within around seven years the body is renewed, the heart is also renewed. The heart that I carried in me eight years ago is not there anymore. It has been completely renewed by what surrounds the earth— by light. Your heart is actually compressed sunlight, and what we have taken in as nourishment has only given us the necessary strength to concentrate the sunlight. All our organs are built from our light-surroundings. All that we eat, all that we take in by way of nutrition, affords only stimulation.

The only thing that food does give us is that it builds a kind of inner chair, in which we feel ourselves, as we would feel the pressure against us of a chair. In ordinary life, as a result of this resistance we have the feeling of our self, our ego, and this is related to the physical material we have in us. You feel your body as you are constantly pressing upon what you have made out of the cosmos. When you sleep, you do not feel it, because you are constantly outside yourself. You feel your body, for it is like a kind of resting bed that is made for you. In some cases it can be hard and bony and in others it can be softer, but it is really like a bed in which one goes to sleep. Of course you know the difference between a soft feather bed and a wooden bench—we feel a difference as a result of which one we have. However, we also feel in the one condition as in the other that this does not concern the real, essential human being. The real human being is what sits inside of it all. I will explain to you next time how all this is related to higher knowledge.

When people nowadays want to reach knowledge, they do not deal directly with human activity; rather, they concern themselves with whatever it is that their "chair" offers them.

Notes

1 Christian Thomasius (1665-1728), philosopher and jurist, delivered the first lectures in the German language at Leipzig University in 1687.

2 Dr. P. Gruner, Professor of Theoretical Physics, gave the Presidential Addresss, entitled "New Guidelines for Physics" (1922), at the eighty-seventh Founder's Day celebration of the University of Bern on November 26, 1921.

3 *The Philosophy of Spiritual Activity* (also called *The Philosophy of Freedom*). First published in German in 1894 and in English in 1916, this basic work of Rudolf Steiner is currently available as *Intuitive Thinking as a Spiritual Path: A Philosophy of Freedom,* translated by Michael Lipson, Anthroposophic Press, 1995.

4 *Knowledge of the Higher Worlds and Its Attainment.* First published in book form in German in 1909. English editions appeared in 1909 and 1910. Currently available as *How to Know Higher Worlds: A Modern Path of Initiation,* translated by Christopher Bamford, Anthroposophic Press, 1994.

5 Eduard Bernstein (1850-1932), socialist theoretician, writer, and politician who rejected revolution and established revisionism as a moderate, evolutionary path for socialism in the 1890s.

   August Bebel (1840-1913), writer, politician, and cofounder of the Social Democratic Labor Party with William Liebknecht in 1869.

6 The report appeared in the *Basler Nachrichten,* July 5, 1923.

7 For example: *The Dream, Psychologically and Cultural-Historically Viewed,* Wüzburg, 1913.

8 *Pierers Konversation-Lexicon,* Seventh Edition, in twelve volumes, Berlin and Stuttgart, 1888-1893.